Oleander Marriage

Oleander Marriage
by Eleanor Lerman

Copyright © 2025 by Eleanor Lerman

Published by Mayapple Press
362 Chestnut Hill Road
Woodstock, NY 12498
mayapplepress.com

ISBN 978-1-952781-29-2
Library of Congress Control Number 2025939725

Some for Robin, some for Phil

Acknowledgments:
Some of these poems originally appeared in *Crosswinds Poetry Journal, Little Fish Magazine, Love Anthology* (Bronze Bird Books 2024), *Quiet Diamonds* (Orchard Street Press 2024), *The Pink Lily.*

Cover design by Judith Kerman; cover image from iStock. Photo of author by Jeff Tiedrich. Book designed and typeset by Judith Kerman in Callisto MT.

Contents

Mothers and Marriages

A Girl on the Streets	5
Another World	6
Fiddlestick	8
Grief	9
Monday, Tuesday	11
Oleander Marriage	12
Don't Read This	14
Second Life	15
Silver Rings and Golden Willows	16
I Walk Away	18
Spring Recovery	19
The Avenue of Trees	20
The Fermi Paradox	22
The Keepsake Garden	24
The Pony	25
California	27
The Wrecker's Coast	29
Good-bye, Tokyo	30

Menemsha

Another Summer	33
Brave Days, Andromeda	34
Cake for Breakfast	36
Calling All Dragons	37
Joseph Cornell: The Catalogue	39
Margaret's Cottage	41
Roundelay	42
The Soft, Dry Light of Uncanny Beauty	43
The Afternoon at Roni's House	45
The Book of Fevers	47
The Grass of Parnassus	48
The Relevance of Nothing	50
The Imaginary City	51
The Last Report from the Underground	53
Yellow Flowers in Stony Niches	54
The Mysterious Forest	56

Theories About Birds	58
The Word of the Day	59
The Pale Pink Brittle Icy Dawn	61
What Turns Here?	63
Velvet Shoes	65
Witch, Walking	66
Starfish	68
Menemsha	69
About the Author	71

Mothers and Marriages

A Girl on the Streets

All at once, the manic forward progress
        simply stopped.

Looking back, it seems that café life
was the easy part; easy to slip into
the lonely city and make up a name.
Easy to be a girl on the streets

when manic forward progress was
the God-given aim and yet the subject
(as it turned out later) of mockery
by the overlords. The joke is

that this body—my only one!—was
a willing participant. They ordered
decay, and so the body took
a hammer to its own wicked heart.

Then the hammer became
its own reward. It called for nurses
and bandages as if it meant
to do repairs. The argument

raged on for years: was she worth
the trouble or just what the wind
blew in when it blew through
the playground? After all, the wind

is an infidel—it knows no regrets,
and yet, there is another theory:
that she is her mother's child,
the lonely mother who went shopping

and never came home. What she left
behind was a ticket to the infinite and
a hint about how the manic progress
forward should be memorialized:

not tomorrow, my dears and darlings
but if you can bear it, perhaps today.

Another World

Look—

There is the perfumed room in the
downtown hotel, the bed full of
sequins, the gauzy scarves we wore,
the mid-century girls who built
jeweled harpsichords while our
gay boys built clavichords in Soho lofts.

In those days, there was an Egyptian poet
who read Greek tragedies to me in a kitchen
above a garden; it was a rainy season,
a season of mist and flowers, of dreams,
and a silver river flying along the city's edge.

Boats on the river, dragons in the waves,
a slice of moon and shooting stars
outside the open window. In those days,
we carried our cats in pocketbooks and
led our dogs on silver leashes as we walked
into the future every summer morning
because summer was the story of our lives,

because the sky was just a wall,
the clouds were the broken doors,
the contrails sliding by were the story
of the time when lost mothers and
their lonely daughters would
find each other in another world.

However, as all this may be nothing,
just a wish, a summer breeze, you think
it is your right to ask me what I want
from all these memories. What is it
that I believe I am still owed?

Perhaps a glimpse of the moving river
that still moves in my mind where
there is a sky that opens to the feeling

of new mornings, which is what
we fed ourselves on our
poorest days, our days of joy.

Which, as all girls want, should begin again:
the wind that stirs, the sky that moves,
everything that is possible as we
dress ourselves in scarves and sequins
and stride along the hallways of the
new hotel with new money in our pockets.

Outside, every angry inch of
city pavement becomes the landscape
of tomorrow, deep in dreaming
of a way to spend that money
on a new disguise.

Fiddlestick

Oh, I'm in a French mood tonight,
looking out the window at the moon
lying lazy on her back in a tattered
velvet sky and the flowers that bloom
in the rubble of the night weaving
their petals into chains and those chains
into the vast rubble of love.

Oh yes, this is a night for chandeliers,
when I have eyes on the faithless sea
that rises and falls with my endless grief.
Admit nothing tonight: break everything
that can be broken and banished and
let it be known that the heart
is nothing but an old fiddlestick
lying forgotten in the grass.

And yet, tonight this dark house
shudders; the windows allow the
wind free rein of all the territories
of the great and deep unknown
when forgotten footsteps suddenly
are heard again—and a locked
door opens, words are spoken…

Yes, tonight, *words are spoken*
and me, me, with so little left to say.

Grief

What approaches in the night, the endless night?

Not monsters—they are old friends from
a flickering screen: Tokyo dies again,
the nuclear monster stomps back
into the sea and I want to know
where he has gone.
Where is he now?

Then a woman dies in 1964 with only
her cousin to hold her hand.
Lillian. That was the woman's name.
My father is somewhere screaming.
Where is my brother?

Where am I?

Now a cat is yowling in the night.
Now I feel the absence of my dog.

Decades, decades, decades march
on and on and I still don't know
how to recover. God, I am old
now and still I wonder:
Where is she?

If her ghost would appear,
I would learn to talk to a ghost.
Instead, I live in a dark house,
a lonely house with a lonely wind
coming wild through the windows.

She left in winter, but I remember spring:
sitting at the kitchen table, a strawberry
pattern on the oilcloth. Did she love me?
Who can be sure, this far away in time?

And the cat is still yowling in the night.
It never stops.

I can go on writing this forever, but it
won't help. Sunny days won't help:
they are disfigured. Even my body
is disfigured—or so it seems to me.
I don't look like myself anymore,
and of course, that makes it worse.

She was younger than I am now,
and the cat is still yowling.
Morning doesn't help.
Grief was anger once, but
now it is only what it is,
what it does.

And it is still approaching,
sitting beside me. *Lillian,* it says,
and the nuclear monster
howls from the depth of the sea.
It had a mother once.

It knows

Monday, Tuesday

In the small days, hope-worn and irredeemable,
a crust of bread under a bloody napkin is all
you will get, the morning meal in a poor hotel.

On the Monday and the Tuesday, all the worried days
live under doctor's orders and even the demons are ashamed.
They have gathered up their little animals and crept away.
Poor things! Now they can't even get a decent job.

And yet, life lived along the avenues is still
buying all its pretty things in the best shops.
Life parading down the boulevards is still handing out
piles of the new money printed down the hall:
the best medicines, the best drugs, all being readied
for the apocalypse—on Monday, Tuesday, they will
come in every color, every shade of a blue mood.

Aqueous lunar days when the sky was plowed
with stars, days of desire in the dance clubs,
days of luster, days of pearl—when was the last time
you remember our days of paradise? The days
before the demon days of pretty things ran out?

Dust and wind and broken windows: now
every day is a small revenge. The hours
used to cost a fortune but Monday, Tuesday,
can be bought without a prescription. Pain is
the new money of the apocalypse and only
old women are allowed to spend it in the shops

because that's what they do when no one
is looking, what they buy with dust and wind,
what they hear when they hear demons' voices
piling up behind the door that on Monday,
Tuesday, is left unlocked at the end of the hall.

Oleander Marriage

> *"[Q]uantum entanglement means that aspects of one particle of an entangled pair depend on aspects of the other particle, no matter how far apart they are or what lies between them...Albert Einstein famously called the phenomenon 'spooky action at a distance'."*
> —Andreas Muller, Astronomy, *10/7/22*

Late at night
mysterious men keep arriving.
They wear the requisite trench coat
but their faces reference modern
portraiture (tight lips, Italian sunglasses),
and when they speak there is a sound
in their voices that is one quaver
above an undiscovered theory of relativity.

Thus armed and thus prepared, they say
they have the evidence to prove that time
is still an appropriate measurement of the
days and nights I turned away from you.
But so what? I have the evidence—
the documents, the photographs, the
scent of oleander and seawater on
our clothes—to prove that this marriage
still remembers to take place.

These men (or women, or travelers
yet unknown)—I think they represent
the fear above all others, that disruption
will come out of nowhere, hide the sun,
upend the moon and stop the tides,
which is, in fact, what has happened now.
You say that you do not know me;
you claim that your life is taking place
in another realm

and I wish, for your sake, that was so.
But what has proven to be simply
spooky action at a distance, whereby
there is no escape from how we affect

each other, you and me, no matter
how far your car can travel in miles or
milliseconds, is actually an entanglement,
a marriage that cannot—will not—be undone.

So into the black hole we go together,
over and over you and me, still brides,
still skeletons, still believing that
there is an inside/outside where
every tiny distance does not—
will not—expand into a mistake.

Don't Read This

It's all over now.
I can't even sleep through the night
without the night breathing down my neck.
You think the sky was hard to fathom yesterday?
Well, today it keeps coming closer;
each star is an eye afraid to blink.

The houses of the zodiac spin around and around;
wheels of fire roll through this house
and I just watch them. I don't care what they do—
they are no match for me.

Because me, I keep the elements of time
in a shopping bag beneath my pillow
so my dreams won't tell me what I
don't want to know. Time, dreams—
if nothing changes tomorrow, I will feed them
to my dog; they are as easy to swallow
as pain pills on the days when pain pills
shake my hand and laugh. Do you hear me?
They laugh.

So you don't really have to read this:
the best way to tell you how I feel
would be to watch a monster
slowly rising from the deep.

Second Life

In the Third Age, it is a foolish dream
to want a second life, but impossible
to stop wanting—and not a city life
of factory jobs and widowed grandmothers
installed in tenement rooms, weeping
as the girl I was walks down into
the subway, to walk up again into
a soaking morning: wet shoes,
wet world, dodging the wind that
scours the city with waste and grit.

Instead, let me take my brother's hand
and lead him down a sunlit road
as if into the tales told by a farmer's
dog in a library adventure book.
Green meadows forever, clear
running creeks, bluebells, phlox
and Queen Anne's Lace—all the
lovely, lazy country too far away
to make an escape for sister and
brother already late for school.

I hear the train on the high tracks
outside my bedroom window when
I was a child—it's night, the train
rounds the last turn and its steel wheels
shoot sparks of golden fire beneath
the only moon I saw. I will ride
the train soon, downtown to the life
I led. I went where it took me.
What else could I do?

Silver Rings and Golden Willows

It lives alone these days, the vagrant heart,
        weakening, growing older.
It listens from inside the body's cage
        but hears nothing.
Love has fled the vagrant heart, which can
        only nibble on thin air.
It asks, but receives nothing.
Love has fled and taken everything away:
the golden scarves, the silver rings, the emerald
        essence of sleep in a lover's arms.
Poor vagrant heart: it has no idea what it did wrong.

It would weep among the willows if willows
        it could find
and transpose the sweet days, run them backwards.
There is the first meeting, the final kiss, the push
and pull of a long marriage that lengthens
        into nothing.
Time is a quantum movement no one understands,
least of all the vagrant heart, which has no home.
Even its loneliness is homeless: the body would like
        to scratch it out, toss it away.
They are at odds now, flesh and heart. Refusing to meet,
they suffer separately: cut and quartered with anxiety,
they bleed alone.

Nothing prepares you, whispers the long marriage
as it watches everything it ever wanted
        walk away.
I cannot live, it says, but knows that it will have to,
each morning dull and empty, each evening pounded
        into bracelets of anxiety
that bind the hands of love, hold them over
        an open fire
that will burn forever, like golden willows
        forever aflame.

So she lies down upon the wind and lets it carry her
        nowhere, everywhere.

She who lived in a great house now wanders
        the vagrant streets.
I will come home someday, the wind whispers
        as it lays her down again.
But no one comes home. Doors open and close
year after year while she waits for what is missing
        to explain itself.
Yes, explain to me, begs the long marriage as the
        telephone rings and rings.
The sound without mercy as it pours itself out
        onto the floor, into the future
as if it was just something she imagined, one last
guess about time and memory, schemers both,
their lies like kites borne away forever
        in the vagrant wind.

I Walk Away

So now comes the last light of afternoon,
the long looking back because too much
has happened, though little was accomplished.
Perhaps that's all there was meant to be.

Though certainly, I can picture myself
as a seeker on a journey, a wanderer,
a rebel, a worker, a victim traumatized
by the rise and fall of civilizations—
or just a passenger, passing by.
Is there any truth to these imaginings?
Who knows? Certainly, not me.

I was born. Someone raised me.
Someone paid for my education,
though I am not sure I ever used it.
I have a passport so I must have traveled,
I have money so I must have paid.
I have a house, so I must have lived here.
I must have lived somewhere, once.
I must have passed the time.

But when all is said and done
there are rules that still apply:
the great estuaries will reek of extinction,
the fatal messenger will arrive too late.
Cities will build themselves without their daughters,
even as I grow too old to be a daughter
so I will have to be something else:

Stars grind beneath my skin.
I swallow the wind.
I am young again.
I walk away.

Spring Recovery

Although I am a city girl (all right: too old
to be a girl, but let's pretend), I want to
walk through country fields again,
drive up to the mountains, to a hidden lake
as blue as silver, as silver as newly
minted coins. I was there once before
and saw an eagle flying low across
the water. I thought, then, it was a
lovely sight. Now I think it was a miracle.

Now, the searing pain of mind and body
reflects the deckle-edged photographs
of my grandmother: Fannie, in an
old summer dress flying around her
in a chain of polka dots—blue and white,
with the ocean in the background,
not a mountain in sight, not a field
of golden flowers and yet, everything
matches in my memory. Even my cousin
racing by on his bicycle—these are
all miracles. I just didn't know.

Now, I crawl over to the medicine cabinet
and select the menu for today. Afterwards,
I open the shades, I see sunlight on
a new street with a new name. Houses,
buildings, cars and vans fly by
and crows alight on the backyard fence.
I will speak to them in the afternoon.
I will ask them where they are going,
how long I can hope that they will stay.

It's a dark season but I will ask for
a spring recovery and try to decode
the signs, decipher what chance they
give me before they fly away.

The Avenue of Trees

Women with European accents
lit cigarettes with delicate hands;
no one ever thought of questioning them
as they walked along the Avenue of Trees.
Wasn't it so beautiful, how the trees bent down
to listen to their whispers, their remarks?

That happened long ago
or it happened in a dream—

Either way, the image contains the antecedents
of everything that followed afterwards,
including why I left home with all the
invisible baggage I could carry and a belief
that my work was as good as a religion
and that love would come in time—love
that would provide a shelter in the rising dawn,
in a sacred grove, a humble place of solace.

But as you have surely guessed,
my dears and darlings, I was wrong.

So many bonds have been broken since
the time of avenues, of quiet walks,
so many desires rotted like old wood.
Now the trees only listen to the wind
that bends their branches, and they
refuse to say what they are told.

Yet here am I, still believing that
somewhere there is a box made of
willow bark and planetary particles
that holds a message someone
needs to read to me.

If you know what it says, please
call me on any invisible telephone
that will be made available in time.
I still need to share these dispatches

with my mother, who was a woman
with a European accent; it is
my belief that she carried cigarettes
in her purse, and everywhere she went
the trees burst into flames

The Fermi Paradox

"Where is everybody?" Question posed by physicist Enrico Fermi, considering the countless stars in the universe with Earth-like planets that might be conducive to the evolution of intelligent life.

Oh, what I would like to do right now
is to go swimming through the stars—

though that, of course, is just
a literary construct, a string of words
meant to evoke a sense of peace—
or perhaps, escape.

Instead, this afternoon I will
end up in the kitchen, plowing through
the piles of dishes, the useless knives
and forks, trying to decide between
candy and nutrition,

between chocolate and carrots—
so chocolate it is. Chocolate rabbits,
marzipan frogs are my witnesses
assembled here as the years

slide around the kitchen:
the years of apartments up the stairs,
down the narrow hall, of running around—
then the marriage years, the years of travel

through an empty world.
And it was empty, or so I think,
with just hints of perfume in the air,

the rustle of silk in a lonely forest
(a sunstruck forest, where towers
of light glimmer like handshakes,
like friendship in a lonely place).

And there are silver mountain peaks,
valleys touched by frost—
ice wheels rolling through the stars,
through fields where only planets play.

So let me finish this bit of chocolate,
then I will open a door or
peer through a lonely window

and perhaps this phase,
this infinite rhythm will slide by
in a party dress, carrying a
secret scroll and a surprising answer—
or not. Most likely not.

But still,
as the days and nights wrap up
in all their infinite splendor
I can't believe it's time to go.

The Keepsake Garden

In the sweet air scented long ago
before personhood was an issue,
there was a way to walk alone
as a simple child in a simple city—
brick buildings, playgrounds, mothers
in summer dresses; sturdy women
walking through the world with
the idea that they would live forever
or so they told us, you and me.

But walking past the keepsake garden
of graves and grief, you were the one
I took with me into the drug-and-
dreamscape city of paisley and guitars.
Incense in the morning, hot streets,
bandanas blooming in the park.

But now there is a dark bird
spread-winged above the city where
once she walked into the cool vestibule
and turned the key; she turned the key
and in the years to come I lay down
upon my bed. When the dolls in the corner
spoke to me, all the blame undid itself.

Children. We were her children when we
were here. But in the years to come
the house cools down; it is a summer evening.
Lightning in the distance knows everything
about us. Outside, in the keepsake garden,
she appears to me as if, in the pictures
of her childhood, she is already laughing
as she learns to speak our names.

The Pony

When I was a young woman
visiting my brother in an upstate valley
where I was a stranger in the rural cold,
I stepped outside and saw a farmer's field.
Snow stretched to the tree line and in
the great black sky the moon rose slowly:
thin, white, sliced like a broken pearl.
Do you live here now? I asked
my brother, and he said, *Yes.*

My brother loves his wife, his child,
the bounty of the world. I don't understand,
but he reminds me that once we lived
at the edge of a park carved out of fields
and swamps by the municipal authorities.
It was a district of Jews, of
secrets and unspeakable distress.

And yet, even we had a father once,
and a mother. The father reclined as in
the Passover story; he listened to the radio
in solitude. Down the street there was
a cemetery often visited by swans.
The mother died. In my mind, she is always
walking away, swinging her purse
even though I know that can't be true.

Can you see me at my desk now,
writing all this down? I hope so.
I hope that as time grinds on
goldenrod still appears along the road
and berries still ripen on the vine.
Tell me that is true. Tell me
that there is, indeed, a road.

In that field, there was a pony
standing alone in the snow.
The farmer came and coaxed him

into the barn so he would be safe
from the treacherous night.

My God, my God,
this is all an enigma.
An unopened letter.
a message that next time
I dare not miss.

California

The time for taking off and heading to California
is past—so long past
that I can barely remember why we wanted
        to go (which is a lie).
Besides, I don't have the right clothes anymore,
and I don't know anyone in the movie business.
Writers who used to be comedians, producers
with shady connections, actresses who pretended
        they could speak French—
they are all back home with their liquor and
        their medicine
or they're dead. Maybe everyone is dead by now.

Even the boys who used to come to clean
the pools for five hundred dollars an hour—
        the coked-up boys
who ate all the food that the actresses and
their spiritual guides left out for the children
        before they took off
for Ibiza, Goa—all the stops along
        the hippie trail—dead.
Doornail dead, or so it is surmised.
All day, all night, the hot, dry wind
        swept through the canyon
but no one answers the phone there anymore.

So the time I could have left for California
in a rented El Camino that would probably
have been abandoned in some burned out arroyo
        outside Silver Wells, Nevada,
went by while I was doing something else:
trying to score on East 10th Street
        or throwing the I Ching
while someone went out for coffee.
(That is a lie—we never left the hotel;
        we lived
like vampires when we lived in the east).

Just chill, you said, but I think that was
        in 1969.
Now the power keeps going out in the middle
        of the country
and nothing happens in New York these days
except that some people are making money—
        mostly men,
and they aren't the only ones who can tell
that the time to have taken off for anywhere
        was last seen
wrapped in a bloody sheet, trying to hitch a ride
        on the Mother Road
as if there were dreams that could still come true.
Chillax, you said, but I think you said that
        yesterday, and I bet
you will still be saying that tomorrow.

The Wrecker's Coast

Morning dreams are a bad business:
they drag me down the wrecker's coast
with two good legs and a strong back,
which they force me to imagine
as if there was something left to
salvage from the mess I've made,

or if I did not make it, as claims
the Ouija board (suggesting reckless
demons), then who should I blame?
And where, now, should I go?

In evening dreams, the subway
rocks and rolls its way back to
my mother's house so I can ask her
why she came here, what she thought
would happen when the war was over
and her mid-century dreams of joy
and recreation came to a final close.

In the end, she says, all the
beautiful clothes, all the incense,
the art and the romances will count
for nothing once you are hospitalized.
But if you can ever crawl out of there,
then whistle for your dog and head
straight for any available horizon.

Keep a dog, a dream, a plan of escape:
that's all your lonely ghost will need to know
about the way to find what's left of any
available eternity, which is what
any mother would tell her daughter
if she had the time to tell her how.

Good-bye, Tokyo

My father believed in television,
so five nights a week I sat inside the glow
as the King of All Monsters marched
into Japan. His radioactive heart burned
like a fiery apple; his eyes were electrified
with poisoned love, which I believed in.
He ate a subway, swallowed men and women
like the appetizers fate meant for them to be.
In my mind, the pressure of his rage was
equaled only by the absence resounding
through a house without a mother.
So good-bye, Tokyo! What do I care
as I go stomping through the years,
still certain to confuse the sound
of a monster's feet behind me for the
lesser encumbrance of flowers falling
as I am running for my life.

Menemsha

Another Summer

Come, sit with me.
Drink your tea, eat your apple
and I will show you my old notebook.
I never finished anything I wrote there,
but perhaps now is the time for me to try,
if only to recover from my old malady.

In the cold, gray morning
I hear the bare winter trees
clearing their throats outside my door.
They are polite, but only symbolic—
they bend beneath the windy sky
and act as if they love me,
but I don't believe they do.

You say you've heard that I've
grown older, and it's true. I count
the cats that come and go, the birds
that pull a summer's worth of clouds
behind them, as if the clouds were memories,
as if the wind could break the back of time

or tumble down tomorrow, carry away
time's nimble burdens. Cold, gray hours
that sizzle on the stove: perhaps I should try
to write about how hard it is to watch them burn.
It's hard, she wrote, *to watch them burn.*

Before the summer ends, I will write to you,
and if there is another summer
I will try to write again, but only
if the wind bends my way,
if the trees, at last, bear fruit.

Brave Days, Andromeda

Café life, city life—
brave days, Andromeda!
Even myths and galaxies took note.
Oh, to be young, to have a young modern life
to waste, and to lie about in dressing gowns,
to rot in a dressing gown with cigarettes
in every pocket. To sleep in hotels
while the city opens every avenue to you.
Lights! Redemption! After brutal nights
and brutal coffee, all seems possible.
Am I right?

Because a young modern life appears
in every movie; it buys its clothes
by speaking Japanese, travels
where it chooses just by breathing,
because its breath is full of stars.
And yes! Sacred bells ring and only
pretty girls are born when a young modern life
parades the boulevards in high heels made of glass.
Click clack, click clack.

Is it not so, Andromeda?
Last year we believed in mythology;
this year, monsoons and fire are all the rage
and rage itself may make an unplanned appearance
when, at last, pain slips into the picture.
So picture this: suddenly, everything hurts.
Every bone begins to click and clack,
the skin peels off the body, lips speak
of poison. Murder and bad dreams.

Click clack. But be brave, Andromeda!
Your story ends when you are rescued,
but who knows when that will be?
Next year medicine will cost a fortune
and an army of saviors may not know
which rock to climb. Next year
we will try again to get well, to use

lipstick and find all the hotel keys,
though next year—if there is one—
may not end with mythology;
in this story, the hero may come
dressed in city clothes with his dragon
on a leash, murmuring that all is well,
all is well, as if nothing had ever happened
and no one really knows how to tell the story right.

Cake for Breakfast

Years ago—many years ago—
when I was young,

I was driving north, towards
a busy city, my busy life.
It was a hazy morning, early,
when I stopped at a lakeside stand
to buy cake for breakfast,
oranges for lunch.

Behind the counter, a girl
as young as I was handed me
what I had bought; nearby,
ospreys flew across the lake,
great raptors, kings of the
fishing birds. It was summer;
heat rising from the water,
mist dripping from the trees.

I told her I was driving home;
she told me that in the autumn,
she was going to go traveling—
to borrow her brother's car
and his hunting dog and head
west, across the Great Divide,
and I believed her. I believe
her still, that come September,
she was gone.

For me, whether true or not,
that is a perfect story.

For me, I know no other way
to say that time does not care
about a morning we remember,
nor will it stop as we gaze
across a lake, while the light shifts,
then changes when the king
of fishing birds finally catches
its prey and flies away.

Calling All Dragons

Look, I understand—
there is a price to pay for all the
downtown days and nights, the way
we assassinated even the rumor of
passing time; the music blocked out
everything, so did the psychedelics
and the conversations about philosophy.
We talked and talked while our bodies
walked along with us—just passengers
doing whatever we wanted them to do.

So I understand why the darling girl
has to be packed up and sent away.
This morning, the hand—this hand!—
that writes these words presented itself
as a victim of essential tremor
as if it was *essential* that my instability,
embodied by the midnight owls that
stare at me with fevered eyes, become
one more factor in my disease.

But even if I understand, still,
the good-hearted soul that has
been my masquerade is furious—

What I want is to call the dragons from
their riverine retreat of green water and
electric snakes—let them dry their
diamond scales and fly to me. *Fly!*
If the world of broken bodies and
half-blind eyes is all that can be left
to me, then burn it—set it on fire
until I hear the dragons bellow.
I don't care if nothing survives.

But of course, I understand myself
and in the end, I would limp out
of my hiding place and tell the dragons
that they were now my pets (though

how I could afford to feed such beasts
is one more thing I did not plan for).
So look: what can I do? I am just
one more child who did not have a destiny,
who arrived here on my own, able only to
take what is left to take from the final
aching days, as if the fate of my poor body
could still break a dragon's heart (all gold
and glitter, all the stories ever told).

Oh fancy nights! I loved everything
about you, but now, only small good-byes
head off into the distance where not even
imaginary footsteps can help me find my way.

Joseph Cornell: The Catalogue

Or, notes on From the Slipper of a Sylphide, *Joseph Cornell, 1949*

What happened was
that he fell in love with a Russian ballerina
he would never meet, not in this lifetime.
After that, he moved to Utopia Parkway
and began to build his dioramas:
a cut-out owl, a string of beads,
the Medici princes, blue vistas,
radical elements of loneliness.

To me, all this exists in relation
to the summer that Sandrine and I
dug up the dying garden on Perry Street
and built a patio, laying bricks in a
mandala pattern. Sand, hammer,
cheese sandwiches and iced tea.
She smoked cigarettes, I took psychedelics,
which made me happy: I thought
we were building a road up to the sky.

In general, I do not ponder the inscrutable;
my memories are specific, not strange—
at least, not as strange as I had hoped they'd be.
No velvet vampire cloaks,
no rainy summers to serve as omens,
no visits from the dead, though I
would welcome them now.

In 1972, Sandrine laid out every print
of every box and diorama that the old man
ever made; on the trestle table in the carriage house
on Perry Street we spoke of metaphysics, drank wine,
tried to understand the art that went into the catalogue
and thought we had already made time stand still.

To me, all this is reason enough to struggle on.
Or maybe not? Sometimes the things
that I remember aren't true, or at least

not enough to fill a catalogue, and yet
I remember everything that happened,
every brick, every owl, every print
we scrutinized, hoping to better understand:
was he in love or was he just dying?
As we are all dying, still happy enough, though,
still willing to take a chance.

Margaret's Cottage

Dark heavens, troubled roads,
moody women staring out the window
at bare-boned skies derived from dreams
that cannot be interpreted—

that is what I know now, that is
what I see. But when I wake each
backward day I always think that I am back
in Margaret's cottage where the sheets
are fresh as early morning and spring
is rising; verdant, fragrant, in every
cup of coffee waiting in the kitchen.

Is it too much to ask to start
all over again? The tarot says yes,
so do the zodiac and all the herbs
whispering in Margaret's garden.
So I take the pain pills, open the shades
and let the year—this year—play
itself out as if it were the first or last.

No one believes me anyway
when I try to explain in another language
that the golden days march on and on,
beautiful and blind, with nothing
to say to any of us. Not a word, not
a clue. Never. Nothing at all.

Roundelay

Trouble occurs with certainty, small joys
        from time to time.
This occurs to me as I remember how
in childhood's school we were taught
        to sing a roundelay:
one voice, two voices, many, rowing
        our boats along the stream.

This year, next year, I wonder if a roundelay
was meant as a later antidote to loneliness
        and to the evil clock
that lights up at two a.m., as well as to
        the teeth of mean discoveries
(aging into a stranger's body, walking with
        painful steps in broken shoes),
that bite with jagged teeth all through the
        morning and into the afternoon.

But still—one hopes for a different message
        to come through,
an extension of a painless hour's peace.
One lifts a loving dog onto the stranger's lap,
        sits on the porch
in the rose-gold evening as an adult's music
        plays in the lonely rooms.
One—she, me—still expects the tune to change.

Someone calls, someone familiar passes by
        and the evening lulls itself to sleep.
She dreams; the dog dreams and they walk
where walking is prescribed: into time,
        along a gentle river's path.
Perhaps the clock, too, can learn to dream.

The Soft, Dry Light of Uncanny Beauty

The soft, dry light of uncanny beauty
sends stars to wander across the daylight sky
to be the things that no one sees
that no one knows

says she, the chatelaine of nowhere
dressed as a Bedouin
dressed as her own death
dressed as an invisible color
alone in this life
aching with life

says she, who has a story to tell
about a broom, a house,
a lost child who may be only
a memory of urban decay,
of where she lived in her first house
in the first city, in the time
of love and love and love and love

says she, but now the soft, dry light
of uncanny beauty will shine no more;
instead, her grave will be a diorama—
one bone, one button, one ribbon,
one ring—or so she says.

Little cats and dogs will pray for her,
little stars will bracelet themselves
upon her memory and she will adorn herself
with silver sighs and silver shoes
and walk down lanes of music,
walk across the three-banked rivers
and open the doors to her first house

and cook a meal: one can of soup,
one flowerpot upon the table, one good day
that will come again—or so she says, when

one good day in the soft, dry light of
uncanny beauty will be when she wakes and sleeps,
when she is good and brave, strange and serene.

Now read all this and ask yourself:
where do you think she went?
Where is she now? If I say she is
still wandering, will you say
she is lost to the rhythm of time?

If so, let the stars keep her secrets.
Secretly, let the little dogs laugh.

The Afternoon at Roni's House

We argued about coming here: one claimed
to be too tired, the other, in a certain mood—
too thoughtful perhaps, too ready to find
a remedy in rescuing some abandoned object—
weighted her insistence with the reminder
of a favor owed. And so, we went to the sale
at Roni's house, her name inscribed
on the mementos she left behind.

*Where is Roni? And why are we encouraged
to pick through her jewelry, her clothes?
Is she hospitalized, never to return?
Is she dying in the sour-smelling hallway
of some senior housing, or is she already dead?*

Those were my worries as we wandered
through the house—an older woman's
house with husband long gone—as I
began to glide (or just pretended so, to lighten
my mood), past piles of dishes, a collection
of ceramic horses, white sheets, pink sheets,
lavender pillows and towels; paintings of
the seaside on the walls, clocks and radios
in every room. Also couches, tables,
chairs, and tools in the basement,
a mess of things in the attic that no one
could ever succeed in sorting out.

This was all too much. Too much for me.

So I escaped: outside, in the back yard,
I looked up to the sky and saw that
something was changing; the wind
was wild and the towering clouds
held each other close: they were
the pillars of an impossible world—
a world where always, death is near.

So I opened a door, slipped back inside
Roni's house. I bought a little clay dog
and a yellow jacket so beautiful
I wasn't sure if I deserved it—whatever
that means. Perhaps it's just an apology for
outliving Roni, or a guess that the jacket
was a gift I would have given to a wild child,
to the impossible girl I was, in the hope
that someday, far from death,
she would remember me.

The Book of Fevers

Chimes in the morning,
wild birds crying in the night.
There are things that don't belong here,
things that are not right.

Open the book of fevers: there are rhymes
that are not recited in the lonely valley,
stories that no one wants to tell, not when
the body holds a knife to its own heart,
being sick of childhood, sick of hotels
and coffee houses, sick of the recidivists
of glamour offering only short-term relief.

And oh, how to stand upon the earth
which is a calliope of bones, of skulls
whose dreams, deep underground,
arrive in an armada of storm clouds,
of wakeful worries without end

said the little dormouse, drinking from
the Alice cup. When once we were
wild with hope, the world was ours;
our rags spoke to us in colors, in
the context of the apples of the moon.
Eat well and drink the night commanded,
misinterpreting our purpose as it
laughed itself out of the room.

So there is the body, still stabbing with
its one good knife as the heart retreats
into its shell. *Everything about being*
born is already known to everyone
said the little dormouse as it stitched
and sewed for all eternity: a dress,
a shroud, a basket to catch everything
that can be carried in a tisket, a tasket,
one last basket of falling stars.

The Grass of Parnassus

There is a field, somewhere
called the Grass of Parnassus,
and even if I can never leave
this poor, deluded house again
I will find out where it is.

But how? How do I live, in this late hour,
rise from my bed of rags
and try to travel one more time?
My heart is in an envelope below the bed
and my only child has gone away.

So I see this picture constantly: sunlight
apportioned into cups that sit on a table
without chairs in a field, long lost,
called the Grass of Parnassus.
Spring approaches but dare not arrive
and my child is gone.

And I babble, I visit doctors,
I hospitalize myself day after day
but nothing changes, never.
The grass grows, the sun shines
with maddening intensity and
still, my child is gone.

It is a gamble, an illness, a loss,
a rumor, a desire, a wish,
an endless journey, a ruse,
a riddle, the shadow of a skull
on a cast-iron plate to even think
about the Grass of Parnassus
and yet, I do. Of course I do

In this late hour, when time
has become an emergency
the Grass of Parnassus has become

a flower that bleeds, a woman
raging through a heraldic sky.
It is the tarot of bad dreams.

It is all that holds up the body when it
rises from the groaning board and
refuses to eat, when it plants itself
deep into tomorrow as a tree
may plant itself in a stony field
and go no further, grow no more.

My child is gone and the curse
that I did not know was upon this house
slowly becomes a classic story
read by a culture already decayed.
So stay awake, poor baby!
Bad things can happen even if
a different fortune was foretold.

I said stay awake!
And when the time comes
(when the grass is smooth and new)—
Run

The Relevance of Nothing

In the libraries of the world
scholars and scientists search
the ancient texts, trying to recreate
the spells of relevance, as if
they mattered anymore.

It would be better to count
the robins and the sparrows
that circle the final years.
There is a loneliness that defies
ambition, no theory that will prove
how not to weep through
all the hours of a summer day.

So open the windows,
let in the rain and the western wind.
Scour the house with radiant forces
and the cold light of the stars.
There are children who will
collect what is left of a woman's
sorrow and carry it home
in a loving cup.

Only the dreams of women
who are too old to leave their homes
are a matter of importance.
Let them wake up in the morning
walking a road they don't remember,
wearing clothes they did not buy

and suffering from nothing
as if their bones were made
of diamonds and their names
inscribed in Hebrew on a seashell
or a feather, with the thought
forever as the only secret
of a chance at forward thrust.

The Imaginary City

Oh, with such gentle hands
the driver helps us slide into the car
and steers us, with such gentle consideration
down from The Peak, across the causeway
heading always to the imaginary city—
the city that belongs to us, to our time.

And oh! The breezes from the east bring
tiny silver birds sailing, shimmering
through the warm and pleasant afternoon.
They bring money with them, and
contented servants. So much better than love!

And so, as in a dream, we wake up again in
the kingdom of glass: the driver takes us
to the floating dock where the silver boat
arrives and we join the others having lunch
at the floating restaurant. We are surprised
by how much time passes so easily!

So much time that dinner is an afterthought
on the ferry to Macao, Kowloon,
the New Territories—all the cities in a book,
the cities of jonquils and cherry blossoms
where we eat, we laugh, we gamble and we sleep:

expatriates doing what we always
wanted, learning to rest and to relax
on an exotic vacation. Everyone is kind
in the imaginary city—well dressed
and gentle mannered. All is well here
All is well.

And thus, our bodies, which once
were lonely, feral creatures, have learned
to heal themselves, to bow and pirouette
as each imaginary face smiles at pretty girls
feeding water lilies to the silver swans

all on a morning that is fresh and new
and wonderful. *Wonderful,* as in a dream.

And in another new-born afternoon
the staff is serving stars dished up with soup
as the music leaves us, floating away note by note,
scraped from the world by the innocents,
the knives and forks of the kitchen chronicles
that we ourselves employ to watch the clock

whose news, we all agree, will be mistaken
(somehow, somewhere)
for the time of death.

The Last Report from the Underground

Cold moonlight poured like water
through cracks in the widows; winter
broke the locks and barged in, banging
up the stairs in hard shoes—it was always
winter on East 10th Street. Rain on St. Marks,

rainy days on the crosstown bus to nowhere.
The Vietnam days. I was a girl when girls
knew nothing, when all the boys looked like
the Jesus kind: black eyeliner, black coffee,
black hearts, because that's what we liked
then, when our own hearts were broken.

Rumors reached us that troubadours had moved
into the Chelsea Hotel, so we flew downtown,
chewing on the ends of our hair. For years,
we waited for a message, but the news from
the prairies never reached us; the papers that we
read were already damaged by conversion therapy

and we wouldn't have believed them anyway—
no one ages in troubled times. No one ever ages
when they walk the streets. Overhead, the sky
kept building itself out of blocks of sun and
clouds and shadows: we stood on the rooftops
and howled at them to come closer and
I think, now, that perhaps they finally did.

But that's not the end of the story—
this is: the last report from the underground
was riddled with bullets. The last time
the East Coast was heard from
it had already crossed the border,
but rumor has it that any day now,
it will confess to how and when and why.

Yellow Flowers in Stony Niches

Whether or not this story is true
it lives in the memory of a wet summer—
yellow flowers in stony niches, black trees
bejeweled with sparrows—when every morning
storms tried to break down the doors of the horizon.
And oh! The sky was gray and gold.
The moon burned all night

but even now, years on, decades later,
centuries (as you see, I am confused),
I have not been told what saved the city
where I lived in rooms above the street
of books and magazines.

And oh! My wild heart,
my ruby, had its own intentions:
it poured blood into the body
and the body used itself carelessly,
as it wished. There was
no turning back then,
no other way

but to wear the disguise of eternal suffering
and walk down dark streets where the body
learned to enjoy itself—
but I think you know that.
You know it still.

Downstairs, someone opens a witch's book,
someone copies out a spell from a
wordless magazine, which means that now
this is a story about the lonely clock
above the lonely bed in the lonely hour.

Well, says the stranger, with one foot already
upon the threshold, *you were young then.*
How could you know that it would turn out this way?

And yet, I feel that I should have known—
as the sparrows flee the trees,
the yellow flowers disappear into the stones—
that something would always
come this way, pretending that
all it wanted was to talk to me.

The Mysterious Forest

Here I am again
alone in the audience
watching the play entitled
*When we hid in the forest
from the shades of night,*
where a classical sense of grief
prevails from dawn to dusk,
where the sky launches an armada
of clouds: heavy, gray,

and when the scene changes
a pale gold silhouette appears
against a pale gold sky.
There are whispers of peace,
whispers that peace may come
on an individual basis
but who knows when.
Or where. Or why

There was a time
when I went about in decorations:
beads and dazzle were what I knew.
Chips of colored glass, necklaces of silver coins.
Oh what a beautiful sight! people would say.
Look at her beautiful kohl-rimmed eyes!
Surely, she thinks about pyramids.
Surely, she will win the day.

But perhaps it was foretold,
in the classical sense, of course,
that the remorseless machinery of time
would bite down hard, would steal
the shoes from all the closets
of the world and march us
barefoot into the forest,

across the waterlily fields,
down lanes lined with golden bullocks
towards mystery destinations

where yes, of course,
I may have a knife in my pocket,
I may have a ticket for another play.
Or I may be lying. You decide:
barefoot across the waterlilies
or onward, into the mysterious forest.
As I fade away.
As you fade away,

and something begins to say
tick tock

Theories About Birds

In the evening
the sky is blue and gold
in rags and ribbons.
In the morning
it is a watercolor
as it has always been.

In the world
there are as many birds
as there are theories about
why there are birds,
when all we can do is make
a cameo appearance: brief,
irrelevant and strange.

Morning, evening, dusk, and dawn:
doors open, women do laundry,
pain breaks the body like candy
torn between the teeth of mountains,
and mountains begin to break the sky.

In the future, a monster—
my monster—
crawls out of a nameless lake
and demands to know
what happened to me.

Please tell him
and tell the others
so we can begin to grow
our feathers and fly away.

The Word of the Day

The Word of the Day, expressed in dreamspeak
just as the dream ends and the day begins,
can change from hour to hour or sink steadily
        into a dark despair.
It is impossible to know what will happen
        she whispers in your ear,
though surely you don't know who she is
or why she wants to speak, these days,
        specifically to you.

If "reverie" is the word today, then
you are spared—for a time—to drift
        in quietude, in peace.
But it could be something that refers to
a wounded woman limping around the house
        in her pajamas.
Too often now, she says, *you think you are*
        two people
and one of them (or both?) is already
        losing her way.

Are there charms, you wonder, or types of witchcraft
that can affect what happens when these words
        slip into the lonely world?
From time to time, she says, *the answer is yes*
        but mostly no.
Apparently no one, at least not now, not here,
is well enough to dress correctly for the weather
and go out to search for antidotes. So there we are.

Sometimes, the Word of the Day decides to
write a clue upon whatever scraps it can find:
        a paper heart, a tissue of tears
or even a telegram that was sent from a different
        source of history
but keeps arriving, year after year, as if it always
knew something about you but was waiting

(in any way of counting,
she explains, *whether in dreamtime or etched*
upon the tiers and towers of the centuries)

for you to be old enough to understand anything
       it had to say

The Pale Pink Brittle Icy Dawn

In the pale pink brittle icy dawn
or in the gloom,
the dry gray heat that signifies
the end and the beginning in which
invisible variations on an unknown theme
mysteriously come to light,
a certain girl refuses to cut her hair
      or get out of bed.
What is she afraid of?
Perhaps I would tell you if I knew.

And if I knew, I might remember
when I was a true believer: art
      meant everything,
no matter that omens could be bought
and sold in the marketplaces of the poor,
      or that the planets
were no longer arrayed in meaningful proportion
      to the lives of women and girls.
Ancient wisdom has become irrelevant;
      it is irrelevant, still.

So come to me, come to me,
in the pink brittle icy dawn
but don't expect me to cure the girl
      who refuses to grow old.
Perhaps she is old already.
I don't even remember her anymore.

So come to me, come to me.
I am the one who needs comforting now,
      strange as that seems.
I need salt for my ruined food, fruit
for the trees that will not bear fruit.
I need so much, O lonely wanderer—
but the old hotels are closed
and art, I hear, has ceased to exist.

And still, in the pale pink brittle
icy dawn
the girl refuses to get out of bed,
so let us leave her to her dreams,
let her be free of art, of pain,
        of poverty.
What else is there to be afraid of?
In the end and the beginning, I think
that now you know.

What Turns Here?

What turns here? she asked.
What turns here, in the outside night
replete with backwards stars?
And the stars turning backwards through
the ether, feeling the pull of deep,
essential gravity—the Om, the ah,
the last leaps of infinity

as if, so soon dying,
she did not care if Christ came calling
or the black earth, voided and bare,
unwrapped for her one last damp bed
but rather, she believed, that the
city streets through which she walked

and all the days and nights of her
beloved catastrophes should seek
to vandalize themselves—rip out
the bloody lampposts, run backwards
the boundary rivers towards the
building sites of all her love affairs

or at least declare an embargo
on the future until its spell is broken.
That is the truth, revealed
in the sly fashion of the renegade—
that what she asked for in the Om,
the ah, she could not have,

not today and not tomorrow,
never in the dancing years,
the to-and-fro of girls and boys
all debonair, all driving towards
the westward edge where the
burning desert of the mid-life mind
meets its match, which is,

she said, as she lit the fire,
hard to swallow, hard to be done;

knowing what is, in fact,
turning out there in the deep
dark night: the debt, the paying out,
the never-ending version
of the long-term cost.

Velvet Shoes

If I could walk through the world again
in velvet shoes, with the lemon-scented wind
as a predictor of better days—
the lemon-scented wind so wild, so wild.

If I could be more poetic
about the bad nights, the days at the races,
the troubled thoughts that infected
the poor body—poor, painful skeleton
clanking along. A rose in the skull,
a blind diamond in each blind eye.

And if I could feel better at sun up,
better in any blue evening than
the one before—if there was no more to lose
as I separate my ancient jewelry from
the pile of ancient jewels, adorn myself
as once I was adorned, inscribed, scratched,
scrawled, knifed and bitten with all
the remedies of fate, the curses of belief—
then this might be a different story.

But instead it is the end of the game,
the one where an angel takes my hand
and explains all that I never knew:
Yes, now and then, yes, cake
and milk, lemons and honey

and yes, at long last yes*: away, away*

Witch, Walking

It's the damp, gray hour
just after dawn. A light wind, hesitant,
not sure yet whether to lay a claim
upon the day.

And here is me: old, getting older,
a woman with a small dog.
A modest dog. I am a modest person,
waking, dressing to take my pet
out into the possible wind.

Also: in this poor county
of women and witches,
it is the hour when the witches
are permitted to walk their dogs;
always, they stay on their side of
the street, I stay on mine.

Here, in this county of
wreckage and grief,
at least this is a safe hour.
No spells are cast, no damage
is done. In acknowledgment,
we wear our traditional costumes:

for me, my old frayed jacket;
for the witch (my witch),
a long black dress, torn in places,
with a dirty hem. And she has
a cloudy eye.

Sometimes she nods at me
and I nod back. Her dog is
enormous—actually, I think
it is a wolf. Red eyes, sharp teeth—
exactly what you would expect.

*Then, as the years go by, I sometimes think
that I hear this animal speak to me.*

In truth, the dog I have now
is not my first dog. This is not
my first witch. And in this life
(the only one), things seem
to be repeating themselves.

And so the house gets cleaned,
the groceries are delivered.
I try to hide the damp gray hours
in the closet, but you know how
the story will be told:

She crossed the street. The faithful
dog followed. But even I can't tell
anymore if I ever went home.

Starfish

In this harsh century
all the skies are old and cloudy
and the wind, when it visits,
does little to appease the shallow heart,
the sad heart, with its thin breath
      gasping in the thin air.
So how do we know, because
so little is known about the weight
of dying: how it stops the rivers
running, settles the mountains
back into the earth and sews shut
      all the roads?
And knowing so little, off we went
into the woods, where even the wolves
      felt sorry for us.
Brave, hardy wolves! They knew
the difference between life and death
is in the counting: one tragedy,
two years, three different selves
bundled into one.
How many more have appeared
since we ate what the wolves ate
      and then traveled on,

traveling because on the other side
      there must be another earth
where the lights stay on all night
      and the sky is luminous.
All the hungry monsters are
      welcome there,
and we will be their children
with a starfish in our pockets,
      all that's necessary
to find our way back to the sea.

Menemsha

The summer I was nineteen
I plied the east coast like a pirate
from Manhattan, bringing you
all the things that you forgot: your drugs,
the dog's medicine, the list of excuses
for the famous actresses you didn't hire
for the movie. It was not an easy job,
being your house slave in the city,
the tenant with a tuning fork and
three white cats. It was a hot summer,
rabid, famished: I thought the house
above Menemsha Pond was an oasis.
In the city, the harpsichords remained
unbuilt: I had to go home to wind
the satin ribbons, bend the golden wires.

I didn't know how much I would miss
the way everything made me angry.

It is unfair to learn too much too young,
to sleep in a high bed with a gun under
the pillow. I rode my bicycle all night
up and down the hills of Manhattan
under a high moon, my soul companion.
I would bite through the years then, hammer
the flat hand of agony that I could have
sworn you said knew how to control
the tides. And the songs played in
my mind, the records spun on and on
in your house in the city while you sailed
across Menemsha Pond and I sat at your
table under a stained glass lamp, plotting.
I thought that I had plans.

So how can you all be dead now in California,
all the handsome men and pretty women
long before I got there, moved my
own house as the crow flies—from the
east coast to the west under a traveler's moon?

I didn't know there were no more movies
to be made, no life to live except the real one.
You didn't tell me how hard it would be
to sit where the darkness grows,
where the angry tides of our Menemsha
exchange their salt for cold clear water
and all I can do is watch.

About the Author

During a career that now spans over 50 years, Eleanor Lerman has published numerous award-winning collections of poetry, short stories, and novels. One of the youngest people ever to be named a finalist for the National Book Award in Poetry, she also won the inaugural Juniper Prize from the University of Massachusetts Press and the Lenore Marshall Poetry Prize from the American Academy of Poets, among other accolades. In addition, her novels have been recognized with numerous awards, including the John W. Campbell Award for Best Book of Science Fiction and being shortlisted for The Chautauqua Prize. Recent awards for her short fiction have included being named a finalist for the Missouri Review Perkoff Prize.

Lerman has also received a Guggenheim Fellowship for poetry as well as fellowships from the National Endowment for the Arts for poetry and the New York Foundation for the Arts for fiction. Her most recent work, *Slim Blue Universe* (Mayapple Press 2023), was a finalist for the Eric Hoffer Medal Provacateur, among other awards. In 2026, She Writes Press will publish *King the Wonder Dog and Other Stories,* her collection of new short stories. Find her online at *eleanorlerman.com* and on Facebook (*facebook.com/eleanor.lerman*)

Recent Titles from Mayapple Press...

Joy Gaines-Friedler, *Secular Audacity,* 2025
    Paper, 68pp, $21.95
    ISBN 978-1-952781-26-1
Ellen Stone, *Everyone Wants To Keep the Moon Inside Them,* 2025
    Paper, 90pp, $21.95
    ISBN: 978-1-952781-24-7
Lisken Van Pelt Dus, *How Many Hands to Home,* 2025
    Paper, 78pp, $20.95
    ISBN: 978-1-952781-23-0
David Michael Nixon, *A Wolf Comes to My Window,* 2024
    Paper, 40pp, $18.95
    ISBN: 978-1-952781-22-3
Zilka Joseph, *Sweet Melida,* 2024
    Paper, 60pp, $19.95
    ISBN: 978-1-952781-19-3
Eleanor Lerman, *Slim Blue Universe,* 2024
    Paper, 68pp, $20.95
    ISBN: 978-1-982781-17-9
Cati Porter, *Small Mammals,* 2023
    Paper, 78pp, $19.94 plus s&h
    ISBN 978-1-952781-15-5
Eleanor Lerman, *The Game Cafe,* 2022
    Paper, 160pp, $22.95 plus s&h
    ISBN 978-1-952781-13-1
Goria Nixon-John, *The Dark Safekeeping,* 2022
    Paper, 92pp, $19.85 plus s&h
    ISBN: 978-1-952781-11-7
Nancy Takacs, *Dearest Water,* 2022
    Paper, 84pp, $19.95 plus s&h
    ISBN: 978-1-952781-09-4
Zilka Joseph, *In Our Beautiful Bones,* 2021
    Paper, 108pp, $19.95 plus s&h
    ISBN: 9780-1-952781-07-0

For a complete catalog of Mayapple Press publications, please visit our website at *mayapplepress.com*. Books can be ordered direct from our website with secure on-line payment using PayPal, or by mail (check or money order). Or order through your local bookseller.

www.ingramcontent.com/pod-product-compliance
Lightning Source LLC
Chambersburg PA
CBHW050043080526
44586CB00014B/1435